Contents

What is a farm?

A farm is a place where food is grown.

Many animals live on farms.

Animals on a farm

Cows live on a farm.

Some cows give us milk.

Chickens live on a farm.

Some chickens lay eggs.

Pigs live on a farm.

Pigs love to roll in the mud.

Sheep live on a farm.

Sheep give us wool.

Some farms have ducks.

Some farms have llamas.

Working animals

Horses can help move cows.

Oxen can help pull ploughs.

Dogs can help move sheep.

Cats can help catch rats and mice.

Taking care of farm animals

Farm animals need food and water.

Farm animals need a safe place
to sleep.

Can you remember?

Which animals give us milk?

Answer on page 24

Picture glossary

oxen cows or bulls that are trained to pull ploughs or do other farm jobs

plough farm tool that breaks up the ground so that farmers can plant seeds

wool hairy body covering on sheep. Wool can be made into clothes and blankets.

Index

Answer to quiz on page 22: Cows give us milk.

Notes to parents and teachers

Before reading

Ask the children if they have ever visited a farm. Do they know anyone who lives on a farm? Make a list together of all the farm animals they can think of. Ask them why they think these animals live on a farm.

After reading

• Sing "Old MacDonald Had a Farm" together. Hold up pictures of each animal to prompt the children to make the correct animal noise. During PE you could put the pictures up on the walls around the hall and when you make each animal noise the children should run to the right picture.

• Talk to the children about page 17. Do they see cows pulling ploughs in their country? What is used instead? Ask them why they think cows and horses are used instead of machines in other countries.

24